BATTLEFIELDS ACROSS AMERICA

ANTIETAM

CHRISTOPHER HUGHES

Twenty-First Century Books

Brookfield, Connecticut

Twenty-First Century Books
A Division of The Millbrook Press
2 Old New Milford Road
Brookfield, CT 06804

©1998 by Blackbirch Graphics, Inc.
First Edition
5 4 3 2 1

Printed in the United States of America on acid free paper ∞.

Created and produced in association with Blackbirch Graphics, Inc.

Photo Credits
Cover and pages 50, 52, 53: ©Antietam Battlefield, National Park Service; pages 4, 6, 7, 15, 16, 18, 25, 29, 37, 39, 46: ©North Wind Picture Archives; pages 9, 49: National Archives; pages 11, 55: Courtesy Department of Interior, National Park Service, Harpers Ferry National Historical Park and Harpers Ferry Center, Harpers Ferry, West Virginia; pages 13, 40: ©National Portrait Gallery, Smithsonian Institution; pages 21, 26, 44: Library of Congress; page 54: ©Ric Durgan/Herald-Mail Pictures; page 56: ©Chris E. Heisey.

All maps by Bob Italiano/©Blackbirch Press, Inc.

Library of Congress Cataloging-in-Publication Data

Hughes, Christopher (Christopher A.), 1968–
    Antietam / Christopher Hughes. — 1st ed.
        p.   cm. — (Battlefields across America)
    Includes bibliographical references (p.   ) and index.
    Summary: Provides background on the circumstances leading up to the Civil War and describes the details of the pivotal battle at Antietam.
    ISBN 0-7613-3009-7 (alk. paper)
    1. Antietam, Battle of, Md., 1862—Juvenile literature. [1. Antietam, Battle of, Md., 1862. 2. United States—History—Civil War, 1861–1865—Campaigns.]
I. Title. II. Series.
E474.65.H84   1998
973.7'336—dc21   97-35270
                                                                   CIP
                                                                      AC

CONTENTS

PART ONE

THE CIVIL WAR:
NORTH AGAINST SOUTH

In 1860, the United States of America was preparing for war. Less than 100 years old, the young country had already fought two wars with England and one with Mexico. The coming war, however, would be different than the previous ones. This conflict did not involve the United States fighting another nation, but the states fighting against each other. It was a civil war, with the northern half of the nation preparing to fight against the southern half.

The Civil War was caused by many longstanding differences between the North and South. The most important difference was the practice of slavery, which was allowed in most southern states and forbidden in the North. Americans had been divided over the issue of slavery since the birth of the nation.

A Nation Grows Up

The United States of America was formed when a group of 13 colonies located on the eastern coast of North America won independence from England in the late 1700s. In 1776, the leaders of the American Revolution issued the Declaration of Independence, which stated their reasons for wanting to be free from Britain's rule. This declaration included the idea that "all men are created equal." It also stated that all men had the right to "Life, Liberty, and the pursuit of Happiness." Equality and rights did not really apply to "all men," however, and certainly did not apply to all people. Those considered to have legal rights under the law were the white, property-owning males—women and minorities were excluded. And although many of the leaders of the American Revolution owned slaves, there was very little talk of ending slavery at the time.

After the colonies won their independence, the Constitution was written. It contained the laws that governed the newly created United States. This Constitution included those laws the leaders considered necessary to protect the freedom and rights of the people of the United States.

< 5 >

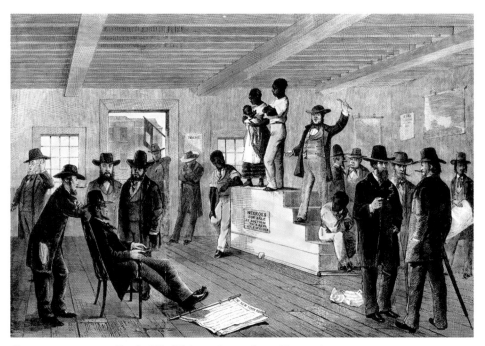

Slaves were not protected by the Bill of Rights and were often sold at auction.

Soon after the Constitution was established, the first ten amendments (called the Bill of Rights) were added to the document. These amendments established a list of rights and freedoms for the people of the United States. These rights, however, were still not intended for everyone—the Constitution did not forbid the practice of slavery. According to the Constitution, a slave was counted only as three fifths of a person when the population of a state was calculated. To some, this meant that the Constitution accepted and permitted the practice of slavery.

Differences from North to South

As the United States grew, the North and South developed in different ways. In the North, the Industrial Revolution occurred. New factories and tools were built and goods that were once made by

< 7 >

hand were made by machines. The factories were usually located in cities, where materials could be received easily, finished products could be sent out, and there was always a plentiful supply of workers. By the time the Civil War began, the North produced most of the nation's footwear, cloth, and firearms. As factories grew larger and more successful, more and more people moved into Boston, New York, Philadelphia, and the other large cities of the Northeast. This population boom fueled the growth of railroads to connect these cities.

The South also experienced great changes. The South's economy was based on farming, and one of the most profitable crops was cotton. The invention of the cotton gin in 1793 allowed southern farmers to clean even greater amounts of cotton than in the past. The growth of this industry led to a southern expansion to the west, where there was more land. Cotton soon became the most important crop in the South. It required a huge work force, made up mostly of slaves. The growth of the cotton trade made slavery seem more necessary than ever to the southern farmers.

Differences between city factories and country plantations were not the only split developing between the

After the Industrial Revolution, many people in the North worked in factories, like the textile mill shown here.

< 8 >

North and the South. The North had a larger population, better transportation systems, and better government services. The South was more spread out and isolated. Although Southern cotton was important to textile factories in the North, as well as in Britain and France, the South was not as economically powerful as its northern neighbors.

There were also political differences between the North and South. The North wanted the federal government to have strong control over the nation as a whole. The South preferred to allow each individual state the right to determine its own major decisions. This division between the nationalist North and the states' rights South continued to cause conflict right up to the start of the Civil War.

Slavery in the Expanding United States

All of these issues became increasingly important as the United States grew in size. In 1846, the United States was involved in a conflict with Mexico over the location of the border between the two nations. The war with Mexico lasted less than two years, and was a clear victory for the United States. As a result of the war, the United States gained present-day California, Arizona, Nevada, Utah, New Mexico, and part of Colorado. This war also produced many of the most important military leaders of the upcoming Civil War, including Robert E. Lee, Thomas "Stonewall" Jackson, Ulysses S. Grant, and George McClellan.

In addition to expansion by warfare, the nation's borders had been expanded by explorers who pushed westward and by such events as the purchase of the Louisiana Territory from France in 1803. As transportation improved and the population increased, more and more people moved into these new territories. Eventually, each territory applied to become a state. One question that quickly

< 9 >

arose in these areas was whether or not to allow slavery in the new states. Northerners favored banning slavery. Southerners wanted the new states to be allowed to choose slavery. Congress, in an effort to satisfy both sides of the debate, made a series of compromises.

In 1820, the Missouri Compromise allowed Missouri to become a slave state, and Maine was admitted as a free state—a state without slavery. In addition, slavery was forbidden in the Louisiana Territory north of the 36°30′ parallel. (A *parallel*, also called a line of latitude, is a horizontal line used to indicate distance from the Equator.) Thirty years later, the same issues arose over the question of California. The Compromise of 1850 allowed California to enter the Union as a free state, and New Mexico and Utah to decide for themselves whether or not to allow slavery. The Compromise of 1850 also abolished trading slaves in Washington, D.C. That same year, Congress passed a Fugitive Slave Law that kept the North from helping escaped slaves. Four years later, the territories of Kansas and Nebraska were both created. And although both new territories were above the 36°30′ line established in 1820, they were allowed to choose whether to become slave or free states.

Dred Scott

Congress was not the only branch of the government that had to deal with the issue of slavery and expansion. In 1857, a case called *Dred Scott* v. *Sanford* came before the U.S. Supreme Court. Dred Scott was a slave whose owner had taken him to

< 10 >

live in the free state of Illinois and in the territory of Wisconsin, which was free according to the Missouri Compromise. When Scott was returned to Missouri, he sued his master for his freedom, claiming that his time living in free states had made him free from slavery. When the case was brought to the Supreme Court, Chief Justice Roger B. Taney declared that, as a slave, Scott was not a citizen of the United States, and therefore did not have the right to sue for his freedom. The Court went on to state that Congress had no right to determine whether or not territories or states permitted slavery— that decision was up to the states themselves. The Court's decision reversed all the compromises that had been established by Congress regarding slavery in the territories. While the South approved of the Court's opinion, the North was furious. The split between the North and South became wider than ever.

A Nation Divided

The question of slavery was not only a political issue, but also a personal one. Some people were opposed to slavery because they thought it was morally wrong to enslave another person. But many people in the South felt that slavery was a necessary and acceptable part of their society. In 1852, the abolitionist Harriet Beecher Stowe wrote a book called *Uncle Tom's Cabin*. This story of plantation life forced many people to think about the issue of slavery. The book was written to challenge the people in the North to do what they could to stop slavery. Abolitionists wanted to make slavery illegal throughout the United States and the territories. Newspaper articles and speeches began to be published by abolitionists throughout the North calling for an end to slavery. Some of these people, however, were not content just to make speeches or write articles. They felt that violence was the quickest way to abolish slavery.

< 11 >

John Brown's Raid

Probably the most famous of these reformers was John Brown. A determined abolitionist from Connecticut, John Brown moved to Kansas at the time when the debate over slavery in that state was raging. In Kansas, he fought against the Southerners who supported slavery, and he and his followers killed five men. In 1859, Brown launched an attack on the national armory at Harpers Ferry in western Virginia. His plan was to create a massive slave rebellion using weapons from Harpers Ferry, and eventually to establish a new state for freed slaves. The slave uprising never happened, and John Brown was captured by U.S. forces led by Colonel Robert E. Lee. Brown was found guilty of treason and murder and was hanged. To many in the North, he had represented a worthy cause, and his death only helped to increase the tensions between the anti-slavery North and the pro-slavery South.

In this watercolor painting commissioned by the National Park Service, U.S. Marines batter down the door of the engine house at Harpers Ferry, where John Brown and his followers were holding hostages.

< 12 >

Horace Greeley, editor of the New York *Daily Tribune*, summed up the feelings of many abolitionists when he wrote,

[John Brown]periled and sacrificed not merely his own life—that were, perhaps a moderate stake—but the lives of his beloved sons, the earthly happiness of his family and theirs, to benefit a despised and downtrodden race—to deliver from bitter bondage and degradation those who he had never seen.[1]

The tensions between North and South were also clearly evident in political battles—especially the 1858 race for senator from the state of Illinois. The Democratic candidate, Stephen Douglas, favored the idea of letting each state decide whether or not to allow slavery. The Republican candidate, Abraham Lincoln, did not think the nation could continue to be "half slave and half free." Their debates were printed in newspapers all over the country. Although Douglas ended up winning the Senate election in Illinois, some of his views were not popular in the South. Lincoln's views, however, won him considerable support among people in the North and made him a well-known national figure despite his loss to Douglas.

Abraham Lincoln Becomes President

Two years later, in the race for president, the Democrats were split—Douglas had the support of the northern Democrats, but the southern Democrats nominated John C. Breckinridge. The Republicans united under Lincoln, who wanted to stop the growth of slavery. With the Democrats split, Lincoln won the presidential election.

Lincoln had never proposed ending slavery entirely. He had only promised to keep it from spreading to new territories. But the South feared that he would eventually ban slavery completely. They were also afraid that he would not support fugitive slave laws, and that slave rebellions, such as the one planned by John Brown, would occur. Many Southerners believed the time had come to secede, or withdraw, from the United States. These secessionists thought that there was no longer any hope for successful compromise between the North and South, and they planned to form their own nation apart from the rest of the United States.

Abraham Lincoln

Moving Toward War

On December 20, 1860, South Carolina voted to secede from the Union. The state claimed that since it had voluntarily joined the United States, it could also leave whenever it chose. Over the next two months Georgia, Florida, Alabama, Mississippi, and Louisiana also seceded. These six states formed a new nation, called the "Confederate States of America" on February 4, 1861. They chose Jefferson Davis as their new president, and declared that slavery was necessary for the economic survival of the South. In March, Texas also voted to join the Confederacy.

Lincoln reminded people that "the Union is older than the states, and in fact, it created them as states."[2] He repeated that his intention was not to end slavery in the states where it already existed, but only to stop it from spreading to any new territories. He also stated that, while he would not launch an invasion of the South, he would protect all government property and services.

This promise to protect government property became a dangerous issue regarding Fort Sumter, which was located in Charleston,

< 14 >

South Carolina. Fort Sumter needed supplies, but one supply ship had already been turned back by guns at another South Carolina fort. Lincoln then had to decide whether to resupply Fort Sumter and risk open warfare, or withdraw his forces from it and accept the presence of the Confederacy as an enemy nation.

Fighting at Fort Sumter

Lincoln chose to send the supplies to the fort. He thought it was better to risk a conflict, which he hoped could be settled quickly, than to recognize the Confederacy. When his decision was announced, the South attacked—even before the supply ship arrived. On April 12, 1861, Confederate artillery began shelling Fort Sumter. The attack lasted for more than a day, and the soldiers in the fort were forced to surrender. Although no one was killed in this first battle, it marked the end of a fragile peace between the North and South— and the beginning of the Civil War.

President Lincoln responded by calling for troops. He asked the Union states to provide 75,000 soldiers from the state militias for a period of 90 days. The North was quick to send the volunteers, but the states in the middle of the nation were less willing. Virginia, North Carolina, Tennessee, and Arkansas all voted to join the Confederacy. The loss of Virginia was especially hard on Lincoln. It placed Washington, D.C., directly on the border of the conflict. It also meant that the best leader in the U.S. Army, Robert E. Lee, would join the South. Although Lincoln had planned to ask Lee to command the Union forces, Lee decided he could not fight against his own state of Virginia. He eventually became the commander of the Confederate armies.

Maryland, Delaware, Kentucky, and Missouri were on the geographic border between the North and the South. If the Union lost Maryland, Washington, D.C., would be completely surrounded by enemy territory. Lincoln sent troops into Baltimore to arrest those state leaders who favored secession, and Maryland voted to stay in the Union. Delaware and Missouri also voted to stay in the Union, and the western section of Virginia broke away and became the Union state of West Virginia. Kentucky also agreed to side with the North.

Residents of Charleston stand on their rooftops watching the bombardment of Fort Sumter.

With the two sides established, the North and the South both prepared for continued fighting. The North had the advantages of a larger population and better transportation systems. The North also kept control of most of the navy. The South had the advantages of better leadership within the military and the fact that they were fighting a "defensive war." This meant that the South did not have to invade the North; it only had to keep the North from attacking and defeating the South at home. The South also hoped to gain support from other countries, such as France and England, who both needed the cotton grown in the South to keep their cotton mills in business.

The people on each side believed they were fighting for a just cause. Southerners were fighting to protect their way of life and for their economic survival. Northerners were fighting to preserve the Union and end the spread of slavery. The war that followed would last four years and cost the lives of at least 620,000 soldiers. It was a war marked by huge battles, which caused more deaths than any other conflict up to that point in U.S. history. It was also a war that divided states, towns, and families against each other—a war that forced the United States to fight for its very survival.

PART TWO

ANTIETAM:
CRIMSON FIELDS

Many people in the North were sure that the region's advantages in transportation, equipment, and population would be enough to squelch the South's rebellion long before President Lincoln's 90-day volunteers had used up their time. These people, however, failed to recognize the South's superior military leaders and Southerners' dedication to a cause in which they believed strongly. While the North was planning on a few short battles, the South was preparing for a far longer conflict.

The goal of the Union was to crush the Confederacy by taking their capital at Richmond, Virginia. To do this, the Union army would have to pass through the Confederate forces that had camped at Manassas Junction, Virginia, near a stream called Bull Run. This was a strategic point where two railroad lines joined, and was only 30 miles from the Union capital at Washington, D.C.

The Road to Antietam

To many people in Washington, this battle was seen as a chance for an entertaining outing. Families came with picnic baskets to watch the battle from the safety of a nearby hill. But what they saw was shocking. Union General Irvin McDowell was pushed back on July 21, 1861, by Confederate generals Pierre G.T. Beauregard, Joseph Johnston, and Thomas Jackson (who earned his nickname, "Stonewall," in this battle). The spectators saw a battle involving 35,000 Union troops against approximately 30,000 Confederates, with high casualty numbers: 2,896 men lost for the North and 1,982 for the South. This Confederate victory and the great loss of life were the North's first warnings that this war would not end quickly or easily.

Over the course of the next year, President Lincoln's 90-day volunteers were replaced following two separate calls for standing armies of 500,000 men. They were to serve for three years. To lead the Union army, Lincoln chose General George B. McClellan. Fighting shifted away from Washington, as the Union commanders decided to strangle southern

Confederate forces led by Johnston and Beauregard were victorious at the first battle of Bull Run.

trade by putting a blockade on southern ports. They also decided to attack the South through the system of rivers in the western region of the Confederacy, especially the mighty Mississippi, that allowed trade and transportation through the Confederate states.

Union General Ulysses S. Grant was put in charge of these attacks, and he was quickly successful. He captured Fort Henry and Fort Donelson in Tennessee from the Confederates, then camped at a place called Pittsburg Landing. There, on April 6, 1862, Grant was attacked by Confederate forces led by General Albert Johnston in what is now called the battle of Shiloh. Although Grant was eventually able to recover from the attack and hold his position, a total of almost 3,500 Americans died and 16,000 were wounded. The Union and the Confederacy both recognized that the fight would now take years to settle.

In the east, the relative quiet was broken by McClellan's plan to once again attack Richmond. Stopped and surrounded by Lee's forces, McClellan was eventually forced to retreat toward Washington. Lee took advantage of this retreat, moving his forces into position to attack Union General John Pope's forces in northern Virginia. At Manassas Junction, the battle called Second Bull Run

< 19 >

took place on August 29 and 30. This was the same area where spectators had gathered just over a year earlier for the first battle at Bull Run. The result was almost the same; the Union troops escaped into Washington with over 16,000 casualties, compared to 9,000 Confederate soldiers lost (killed or wounded).

This Union retreat seemed to offer Lee the perfect chance to improve the South's position in the war. With the Union, or Federal, army recovering in Washington, Lee had a clear path across the Potomac River and into Maryland. Lee believed there was strong support for the Confederacy within Maryland, and he hoped to convince Maryland to secede from the Union.

Lee also wanted to relieve northern Virginia from some of the fighting during the harvest season. In addition, the Confederacy was still hoping for aid from Europe—in fact, France and England may have been close to supporting the South. Lee thought that they would show their support more quickly if he could prove that the South was winning the war through a successful campaign into Union territory.

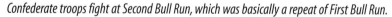

Confederate troops fight at Second Bull Run, which was basically a repeat of First Bull Run.

< 20 >

Lee's Invasion

On September 4, 1862, Lee's Army of Northern Virginia crossed the Potomac River at White's Ferry, Virginia, into Maryland—and Union territory. Some onlookers were unimpressed with his forces. As one resident wrote, "I felt humiliated at the thought that this horde of ragamuffins could set our grand army of the Union at defiance. Oh! They are so dirty! I don't think the Potomac River could wash them clean!"[1] Three days later, Lee captured Frederick. From there, Lee sent Jackson with two thirds of the army to attack the Federal garrison (a group of soldiers based in a town) at Harpers Ferry. This would allow the Confederates to take over the large supply of goods that were being stored there. It would also help to protect Lee's route back into Virginia, if a retreat became necessary. The remainder of Lee's army, under the command of General James Longstreet, stopped in Boonsboro, Maryland, and then moved on to the town of Hagerstown. (An exception was D.H. Hill, who remained in Boonsboro.) Longstreet would try to hold off McClellan, who was in Washington.

Lee's plan was dangerous because he was splitting his army into smaller parts while invading enemy territory. If McClellan attacked quickly while the southern army was divided, he could destroy the Army of Northern Virginia and help end the war. Lee was confident, however, that his army would be safe. McClellan had earned a reputation as a very cautious and slow-moving leader. Lee counted on this and planned to take Harpers Ferry, resupply his army, and unite the two forces together again—all before McClellan became a threat.

Special Order No. 191

What happened next is one of the greatest mysteries of the war. Lee's decision to divide his troops was written out in what was called

Born in 1807, Virginia native Robert E. Lee graduated near the top of his class at West Point in 1829. Lee married Mary Anna Randolph Curtis, great-granddaughter of Martha Washington.

In 1859, Lee led the forces that captured John Brown at Harpers Ferry. When Virginia chose to secede from the Union in 1861, Lee turned down the chance to command the Union's field forces. He resigned from the U.S. Army in order to serve his home state in the Civil War.

Lee replaced Joseph Johnston in command of the Army of Northern Virginia when Johnston was wounded in June 1862. Lee then pushed McClellan's army away from Richmond in a

Robert E. Lee

series of battles called the Seven Days. He followed this with his fight at Second Bull Run, and from there invaded Maryland.

After Lee withdrew from Antietam, he was victorious at both the battles of Fredericksburg and Chancellorsville. He was then defeated when he again tried to invade the North, this time at Gettysburg. The Confederate forces never really recovered from this battle, and on April 9, 1865, Lee surrendered to General Ulysses S. Grant at Appomatox Court House in Virginia. Lee remained one of the South's most beloved figures after the war, serving as president of Washington College in Virginia (now Washington and Lee University). He died of heart disease in 1870.

Special Order No. 191. This order was designed to be given to each of the generals involved. The Army of Northern Virginia then left Frederick and moved out to its assigned posts, and the Union army was able to regain control of Frederick. In a meadow outside the town, some Union soldiers found a sheet of paper wrapped around some cigars. It was a copy of Lee's Special Order No. 191, addressed to General D.H. Hill. When he received the paper from the Union soldiers,

< 22 >

McClellan realized that if he moved quickly enough, he could catch Lee's army divided and unprepared, and could destroy the Army of Northern Virginia. As McClellan told his aides, "Here is a paper with which, if I cannot whip Bobbie Lee, I will be willing to go home."[2]

General McClellan began moving his forces out of the Washington area, hoping to keep the Confederates divided and engage each section separately. He sent General William Franklin to relieve the attack on Harpers Ferry, and trap Jackson's troops there. McClellan directed the rest of the Army of the Potomac, under Generals Ambrose Burnside and Edwin Sumner, toward South Mountain, between Frederick and the city of Hagerstown. Because of Special Order No. 191, McClellan expected to find General Longstreet's troops at Boonsboro, which is on the north side of South Mountain. In fact, the plan had changed slightly, and most of Longstreet's command was about ten miles away in Hagerstown. If McClellan had ordered an immediate advance against South Mountain on September 14, he could have driven the Confederates quickly from Turner's Gap, a pass which cut across the mountain, and controlled the mountain before Longstreet moved his troops. Because he thought that Longstreet was in Boonsboro, however, McClellan was much more cautious. Although the Union soldiers, under General Ambrose Burnside, did eventually take Turner's Gap and gain control of South Mountain, their victory cost them an entire day of fighting. This allowed Lee time to reorganize his forces and develop a new plan.

The Siege at Harpers Ferry

At Harpers Ferry, the battle turned against the Union forces. Surrounded by three areas of high ground in two different states, Harpers Ferry was a very difficult place to defend. According to

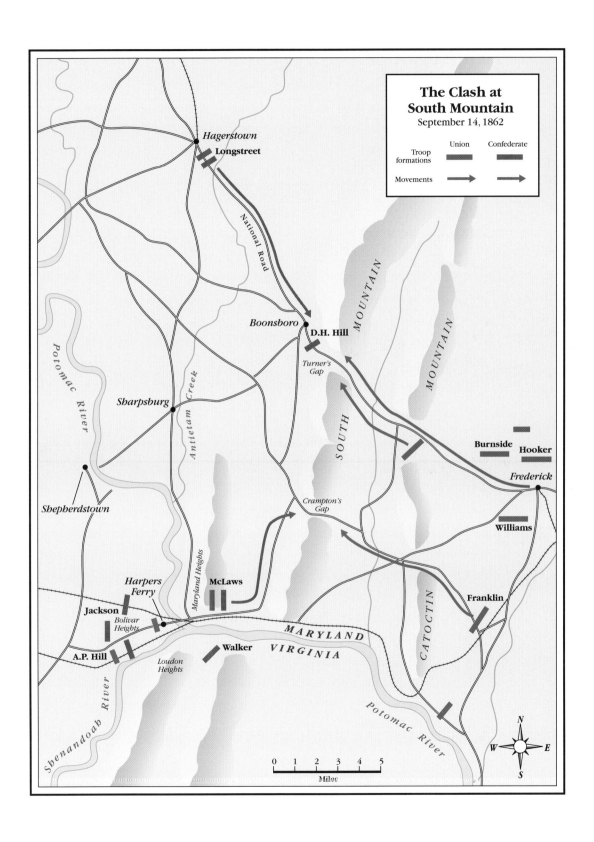

The Clash at South Mountain
September 14, 1862

Troop formations	Union	Confederate
Movements		

Hagerstown

Longstreet

National Road

SOUTH MOUNTAIN

MOUNTAIN

Boonsboro

D.H. Hill

Turner's Gap

Sharpsburg

Potomac River

Antietam Creek

Burnside **Hooker**

Frederick

Crampton's Gap

Williams

Shepherdstown

Maryland Heights

Franklin

Harpers Ferry

McLaws

CATOCTIN

Jackson

Bolivar Heights

A.P. Hill

Walker

Loudon Heights

MARYLAND

VIRGINIA

Potomac River

Shenandoah River

0 1 2 3 4 5
Miles

N
W E
S

< 24 >

Lee's plan, Jackson had further divided his forces into three parts: one to attack from Loudon Heights on the Virginia side, one from Bolivar Heights to the west of Harpers Ferry, and one from Maryland Heights on the Maryland side. Once the Confederates held the high ground on every side of Harpers Ferry, there was little the Union troops could do other than hope for aid from McClellan.

Although McClellan had sent Franklin to relieve the siege at Harpers Ferry, Franklin moved with caution. By the end of the day on September 14, he captured a key crossing point called Crampton's Gap, but it was too late to continue. If he had succeeded earlier, he could have come up behind the Confederates on Maryland Heights and surprised them. Franklin's caution allowed the Confederates to hold their positions surrounding Harpers Ferry; there was little hope left for the Union men inside the garrison.

Lee's Stand

Jackson informed Lee that Harpers Ferry would fall to the Confederacy by the morning. With that new information, Lee sent out orders telling General Lafayette McLaws on Maryland Heights to bring his soldiers to Sharpsburg to meet Longstreet's forces near a stream called Antietam Creek.

The next day, the Federal garrison at Harpers Ferry surrendered. (Franklin had been held up by a much smaller Confederate force and never made his attack.) The Confederates gained over 11,000 prisoners as well as desperately needed supplies. Most importantly, though, the surrender allowed Jackson to march his forces from Harpers Ferry to join Longstreet and Lee at Sharpsburg. Jackson left General A.P. Hill and his division in charge of Harpers Ferry, and Jackson and his men marched the 17 miles to Sharpsburg to reunite the majority of the Army of Northern Virginia.

Born in Philadelphia in 1826, George B. McClellan graduated second in his class at West Point in 1846. Fourteen years later he married Mary Ellen Mercy; they had one son and one daughter.

With the failure of the Union army at First Bull Run, McClellan was named commander of the Army of the Potomac in August 1861. He became famous for his ability to organize and develop an army, as well as his refusal to use that army aggressively. He was loved by his men, because they knew that he would not put them in any more danger than was necessary. The horrible losses at Antietam, however, caused many of "Little Mac's" men to lose that faith in him.

After Antietam, McClellan was removed from command for his failure to follow Lee's army into Virginia and engage the enemy. When he did not

George B. McClellan

receive orders for a new command, McClellan turned to politics. In 1864, he was the Democrats' candidate for president, running against Abraham Lincoln—and he was soundly defeated. McClellan served as governor of New Jersey after the war, and died in 1885.

After Longstreet's forces withdrew from South Mountain, McClellan assumed they were attempting to retreat back into Virginia. He believed he had completely defeated Lee's forces, and sent the same telegraph to Washington and to his wife proclaiming victory: "Have just learned that the enemy are retreating in a panic and

A photograph taken in 1862 shows the railroad bridge at Harpers Ferry, which was destroyed during the Confederate attack.

that our victory is complete."[3] Soon, however, word began to arrive that the Rebels had not fled. Instead they had lined up in battle formations on the west side of Antietam Creek.

On the following day, September 16, McClellan brought his army to the banks of Antietam Creek, but he did not attack Lee's forces. This was another opportunity missed by McClellan, because only about half of Lee's forces were on the field ready for battle at that point. By evening, Lee's force had been completely reunited, with the exception of A.P. Hill's division at Harpers Ferry. Lee had about 35,000 soldiers lined up along a four-mile stretch between Antietam Creek and the Potomac River, three miles away. Jackson was in command of the forces on the left, and Longstreet, those in the center and on the right. Lee had his headquarters near the town

< 27 >

of Sharpsburg. Antietam Creek was not extremely deep or fast; it could be crossed slowly by soldiers, but not by artillery. This made the three bridges along the Antietam extremely important to both sides. The Union would have to use these bridges to get their guns across the water.

Lee had chosen to make his stand in an area of rolling fields and woodlots, dotted by houses and farm buildings. The most visible landmark was a small white church of the German Baptist Brethren, who were called "Dunkers," which stood on a slight rise next to the Hagerstown Turnpike. Antietam Creek wound through the east side of the battlefield, roughly parallel to the Hagerstown Turnpike. The hills in the area made it difficult to get a clear view of any surrounding territory. Two columns of troops could move near each other without one ever knowing the other was present.

Longstreet watched the Union forces arrive at Antietam:

On the forenoon of the 15th, the blue uniforms of the Federals appeared among the trees that crowned the heights on the eastern bank of the Antietam. The number increased, and larger and larger grew the field of blue until it seemed to stretch as far as the eye could see, and from the tops of the mountains down to the edges of the stream gathered the great army of McClellan.[4]

Although McClellan thought he was outnumbered, he was in command of close to 75,000 men at Antietam—more than twice as many as were available to Lee. McClellan's plan was to attack in three stages. General "Fighting Joe" Hooker would attack the Confederate left at first light on September 17. Then, from the south, Burnside would attack across the Rohrbach Bridge on the Confederate right flank—the far right side of the Confederate forces. Finally, McClellan would attack the center with the remainder of his

Union

Ambrose Burnside/	*Joseph Mansfield
9th Corps	George B. McClellan
Jacob Cox	George Meade
Abner Doubleday	*Israel Richardson
Abram Duryea	James Ricketts
Edward Ferrero	*Isaac Rodman
William Franklin	*John Sedgewick
William French	Truman Seymour
John Gibbon	Edwin "Bull" Sumner/
George Greene	2nd Corps
*"Fighting Joe" Hooker/	Max Weber
1st Corps	Alpheus Williams
Oliver Howard	

Confederate

William Barksdale	J.R. Jones
Marcellus Douglass	*Alexander Lawton
Jubal Early	Robert E. Lee
A.P. Hill	James Longstreet
D.H. Hill	Lafayette McLaws
John Bell Hood	Robert Rodes
Thomas "Stonewall"	*William Starke
Jackson	Robert Toombs
David Jones	John Walker

(This chart lists only a portion of the generals who fought at Antietam. An asterisk indicates those killed or wounded there. All together, nine Confederate generals and nine Union generals were killed or wounded in the battle, but not all of their names appear here.)

army. Unfortunately, McClellan made the mistake of positioning his men during the daylight. Hooker's men moved into their positions at four in the afternoon on September 16. This allowed Lee to recognize where the morning's attack would hit. Lee then moved his own men to prepare for that first strike. That night, there was some light fighting in an area called the East Woods, as the two armies prepared for the most destructive clash in the war's history.

The Battle

McClellan's plan of attack began well. At dawn, Hooker ordered his artillery to open fire on the Confederate positions. His goal was to attack from the north, through David Miller's cornfield and the woodlots called the East and West Woods. He hoped to push the Confederates back and capture the plateau where the Dunker Church stood. As the Union artillery opened fire, the Confederate guns answered—many of them were located on Nicodemus Hill—the best high ground commanding the northern section of the battlefield.

The Dunker Church was the most visible landmark on the battlefield.

Morning Phase

On September 17, 1862, Hooker's First Corps began their attack at 6:00 A.M. He had stationed General Abner Doubleday on his right, to attack through the West Woods. On his left, General James Ricketts would lead his men through the East Woods, and General George Meade would command the attack in the center. Jackson was ready for the attack. In addition to the artillery on Nicodemus Hill, Jackson had positioned General J.R. Jones to guard the West Woods, and General Alexander Lawton to watch the cornfield and the East Woods. Colonel Stephen Lee placed his artillery on the plateau surrounding the Dunker Church, and General John Bell Hood kept his division on reserve in the center.

Fighting resumed in the East Woods, where it had flared briefly the night before. Union General Truman Seymour led his brigade into the woods. Seymour's brigade included the Thirteenth Pennsylvania, known as the "Bucktails" because they wore tails of deer pinned to their hats to show off their abilities as marksmen. The fighting was intense as the Bucktails traded fire with a regiment of Georgians. At one point the Pennsylvanians started to break and run, but they were stopped by a young private. This soldier halted the retreat by standing on a hill and waving his hat, shouting, "Rally, boys, rally! Die like men, don't run like dogs!"[5]

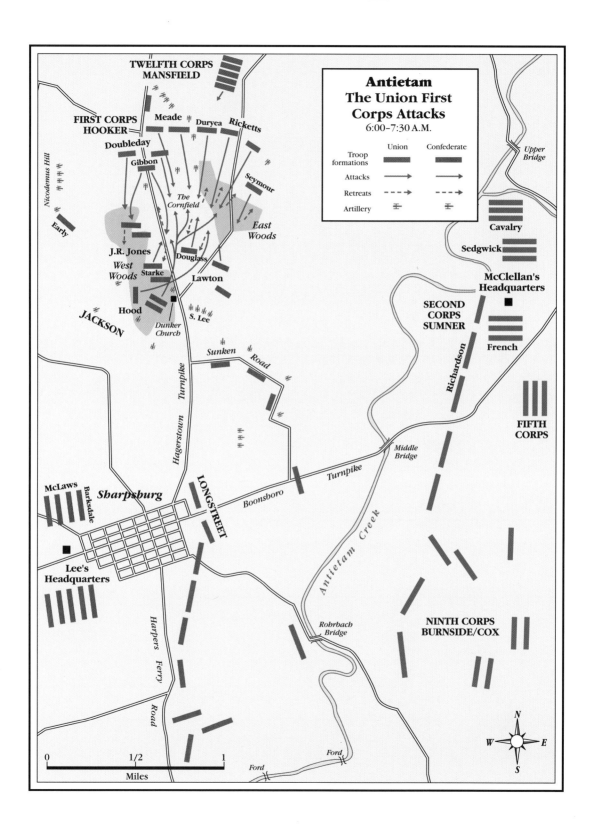

TWELFTH CORPS
MANSFIELD

FIRST CORPS
HOOKER

Meade   Duryea   Ricketts

Doubleday

Gibbon

Nicodemus Hill

Seymour

*The
Cornfield*

Early

*East
Woods*

J.R. Jones

*West
Woods*   Starke

Douglass

Lawton

JACKSON   Hood

S. Lee

*Dunker
Church*

Sunken   Road

Antietam
The Union First
Corps Attacks
6:00–7:30 A.M.

	Union	Confederate
Troop formations		
Attacks		
Retreats		
Artillery		

*Upper
Bridge*

Cavalry

Sedgwick

**McClellan's
Headquarters**

**SECOND
CORPS
SUMNER**

French

Richardson

Middle
Bridge

**FIFTH
CORPS**

Turnpike

Boonsboro

Hagerstown Turnpike

LONGSTREET

McLaws
Barksdale

Sharpsburg

Lee's
Headquarters

Antietam Creek

Harpers Ferry Road

*Rohrbach
Bridge*

**NINTH CORPS
BURNSIDE/COX**

0   1/2   1

Miles

Ford

Ford

N
W · E
S

< 31 >

Rickett's primary attack was led by General Abram Duryea, who took his men into the cornfield—and into one of the most deadly conflicts of the battle. At one point, Duryea's brigade and a regiment of Georgians under Colonel Marcellus Douglass were standing 250 yards apart, firing straight into each other. As one Confederate private described the fury of that conflict, "Never have I seen men fall as fast and thick.... I never saw rain fall faster than the bullets did around us."[6] Although he did great damage to the Confederates, Duryea lost a third of his own men.

To the soldiers who survived the battle, the Miller cornfield represented most of the horrors of the war. This field changed hands several times throughout the course of the morning, and each new attack brought devastating casualties. One of the regiments involved in the fight in the cornfield was the Twelfth Massachusetts. Of the 334 men who went into the battle that morning for this regiment, 224 were lost—including the commanding officer. With its casualty rate of 67 percent, the Twelfth Massachusetts had the highest losses of any Federal regiment for the day. One 16-year-old Union soldier described his view of the fighting:

It was rather Strange music to hear the balls Scream within an inch of my head. I had a bullet strike me on the top of the head just as I was going to fire and a piece of Shell struck my foot—a ball hit my finger and another hit my thumb. I concluded they meant me.... The firing increased tenfold, then it sounded like the rolls of thunder.[7]

Smoke and Confusion

In the West Woods, the fighting was just as intense. General John Gibbon's brigade, in Doubleday's division, marched down along both sides of the Hagerstown Turnpike, pushing the Confederates before

< 32 >

them. As they reached the cornfield, the Union forces opened fire on figures they saw moving through the smoke to their right. The figures were their own skirmishers, who were usually on the flank, slightly ahead of the rest of the force in order to protect it. This type of mistake was common during the battle. The incredible smoke and noise was enough to cause great disorder on all sides. In many cases, the officers who gave orders were themselves wounded or killed in the action, which added to the general confusion. As Gibbon's skirmishers fled the gunfire, the Confederates took advantage of the confusion to attack the unprotected side. Gibbon brought up the rest of his brigade, and pushed on through the field.

The first stage of the battle was tremendously costly to both sides, but the Union forces with their greater numbers were slowly pushing the Confederates back. The Confederates viewed the situation as desperate. General Lawton, who had been wounded and replaced by General Jubal Early, sent a message to General Hood that his support was badly needed.

Hood's men, who were just sitting down to breakfast, responded to the call quickly. His division of 2,300 men entered the battle and immediately began to turn the tide of the conflict. Their first volley against the weary Union soldiers was, according to one officer, "like a scythe running through our line."[8] Hood's men pushed into the cornfield and the East Woods, driving the Union troops before them. Hooker called up the last of his reserves, and sent a message to General Joseph Mansfield, in command of the fresh Twelfth Corps, asking for aid. With his reserves and the aid of the Union artillery firing directly into the Confederate line, Hooker was able to stop Hood's advance—but only at great cost to both sides.

By 7:30 A.M. the two sides were nearly spent. Almost every brigade belonging to Hooker and to Jackson had been used. Hooker himself was wounded in the battle and was replaced by Meade.

< 33 >

Hooker had lost about 33 percent of his men. Those who were unharmed were too weary to continue the fight. Hood had sent seven regiments to fight in the cornfield and along the Turnpike, and had lost almost 60 percent of those men. Later, when asked where his men were, Hood responded: "Dead on the Field."[9] By the end of the first hour and a half of fighting, the two sides that had each pushed the other so far were in positions almost identical to where they had started.

For the Union, Mansfield brought his troops in to reinforce and replace Hooker. On the Confederate side, D.H. Hill brought his troops up from the center to relieve what was left of Hood's shattered forces. Mansfield's Twelfth Corps followed him into the battle, and, almost immediately, Mansfield himself was fatally shot in the stomach. Command then passed to General Alpheus Williams, and he went to work putting his soldiers in the field in place of the First Corps. In the East Woods and the cornfield, General George Greene's division managed to flank the Confederates, attacking them from their unprotected right side. They pushed the Rebels completely out of the East Woods and the cornfield, taking possession of the entire morning's battlefield on the east side of the Hagerstown Turnpike. One Union soldier in the cornfield, fatally wounded, displayed the sort of courage that many soldiers showed that day. He stopped shooting to examine his wound, then said, "Well, I guess I'm hurt about as bad as I can be. I believe I'll go back and give 'em some more."[10] On the west side, Doubleday's forces, reinforced by the Twelfth Corps, pushed into the West Woods and all the way up to the Dunker Church.

Later in the Morning

Again, both sides put in a call for reinforcements. At Union headquarters, McClellan finally decided to commit the Second Corps,

< 34 >

under General Edwin "Bull" Sumner, to the battle. Although General Israel Richardson's division was held back, Sumner led the remainder of his troops through the East Woods to the Hagerstown Turnpike. Lee, meanwhile, had personally arrived to see the situation his troops faced. He brought up two of Longstreet's divisions under McLaws and General John Walker to support what was left of Jackson's, Hood's, and Early's Confederates in the West Woods.

The loss of General Hooker, when a Confederate sniper shot him in the foot, was particularly hard on the Union forces. Without Hooker, General Sumner only had the impression of the battle he had received from McClellan at headquarters, which was a very limited view. Sumner marched General John Sedgewick's division straight across the East Woods to an area he assumed would be filled with Confederates. Sedgewick's men were set up to fight the enemy face-to-face, but Sumner's information was incorrect—the Rebels were farther to the south. This meant they would be along the left side of the Union troops as they marched into the West Woods.

Sumner had unknowingly marched Sedgewick's men into a trap. As Jackson received his reinforcements from McLaws's division, he put together an attack against the left flank of the Union soldiers. Because they were lined up to fight an enemy to the front, most of Sedgewick's men couldn't turn in time to meet the new attack. When they did turn, often the people they were pointing their guns at were other Union soldiers. At one point, the soldiers in the Fifty-Ninth New York opened fire—directly into the backs of the Fifteenth Massachusetts, who suffered a total of 315 casualties from the bullets of both their friends and their foes.

Sedgewick's division was nearly destroyed. The Confederates had taken positions on three sides of the Yankees, and the only possible route of escape was to the north. By the time most of those regiments turned around again to hold their ground, they were all

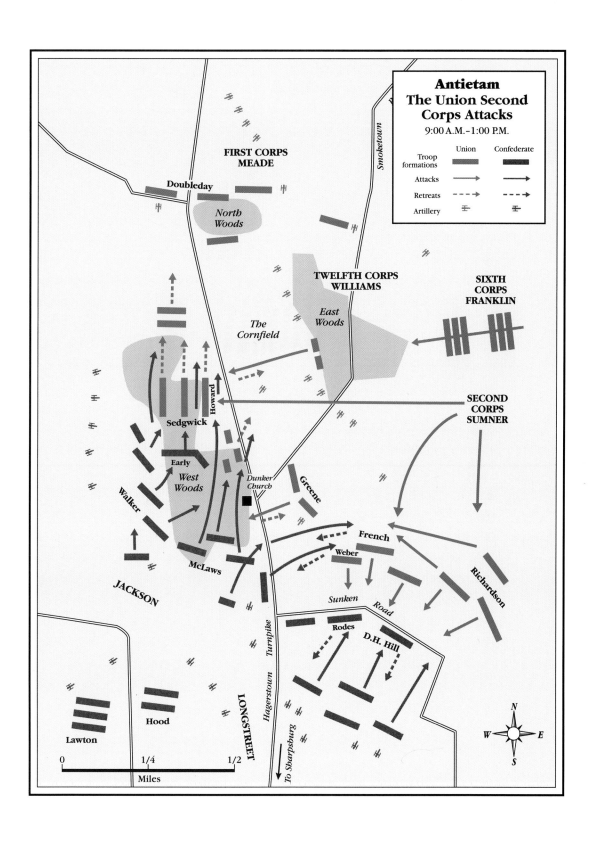

Antietam
The Union Second Corps Attacks
9:00 A.M.–1:00 P.M.

	Union	Confederate
Troop formations		
Attacks		
Retreats		
Artillery		

FIRST CORPS
MEADE

Doubleday

North Woods

Smoketown

TWELFTH CORPS
WILLIAMS

East Woods

SIXTH
CORPS
FRANKLIN

The Cornfield

Howard

Sedgwick

Early

West Woods

Walker

Dunker Church

Greene

SECOND
CORPS
SUMNER

McLaws

JACKSON

French

Weber

Richardson

Sunken

Road

Rodes

D.H. Hill

LONGSTREET

Hagerstown Turnpike

Lawton

Hood

To Sharpsburg

N
W E
S

0   1/4   1/2

Miles

< 36 >

the way back in the North Woods, where Hooker's First Corps had started before the battle began that morning. In addition to all the territory that was lost, Sedgewick's division ended up losing more than 40 percent of its men—more than half of them in the first 20 minutes. General Sedgewick himself was wounded three times before being carried from the battle. After the battle, General Oliver Howard, who replaced Sedgewick when he was wounded, wrote of this stage of Antietam, "the total loss of the division is 355 killed, 1,577 wounded [and] 321 missing…a record of almost unparalleled loss during a single battle. They have poured out their blood like water."[11]

The only Union soldiers to meet with success in this part of the battle were two brigades under Greene, who held their ground facing the Dunker Church and even briefly moved past the church into the edge of the West Woods before being forced back across the Hagerstown Turnpike. At one point, Greene's men ran almost completely out of ammunition, and had to hold their position with fixed bayonets.

Sedgewick's destruction still left Sumner with two more divisions in his Second Corps. Richardson's division that had been held back by McClellan was finally given permission to cross the Antietam. General William French, who had lost Sedgewick in the East Woods, decided to fight along Greene's left flank. Here, at the center of the Confederate line, D.H. Hill had positioned two brigades, as well as some sections of other brigades. They totaled about 2,500 men stationed in an old farm path that had worn a deep rut into the ground. If the Union soldiers could force their way through these brigades, they could capture the center of Lee's field and split Longstreet's forces from Jackson's. The Confederates, however, were in a very strong defensive position. The path was deep enough to keep them below the sight lines of the Federals and the Union men would have to come over the top of an exposed hill in

In this print made from a sketch drawn during the battle, Sedgewick's men are clearly visible as they enter a Confederate trap.

order to attack them. The Confederates vowed "to stay here, General, till the sun goes down or victory is won,"[12] as one officer from Alabama told Lee. The official name of this path was the Sunken Road, but it has become known as the Bloody Lane.

The first Union brigade to attack the Sunken Road was led by General Max Weber. The Confederates waited until they could see the Union soldiers' belts over the top of the rise, then opened fire. Weber's entire front line was dropped—he had over 450 casualties in less than five minutes. Quickly, other Union brigades filled the gaps, but they met with similar results. By the end of the day,

< 38 >

French's division suffered more casualties than any other Union division except Sedgewick's. A soldier in French's division described the approach to the road:

> *The nervous strain was plainly visible upon all of us. All moved doggedly forward in obedience to orders, in absolute silence so far as talking was concerned. The compressed lip and set teeth showed that nerve and resolution had been summoned to the discharge of duty. A few temporarily fell out, unable to endure the nervous strain, which was simply awful...*[13]

As French began to run out of brigades to send into the fight, Richardson's division finally arrived. The Rebels, who were also suffering casualties whenever they ventured out from the protection of the lane, moved in their last reinforcements as well. Richardson sent a brigade off to the southern flank of the Confederates in the road. When the Union soldiers finally gained possession of part of the path, they were able to fire directly down the lane into the sides of the Confederates. Sections of the defenders began to break and run to the rear. At the same time, part of General Robert Rodes's Alabama brigade on the left confused their orders, and began to pull out as well. Richardson's men were then able to cross the Sunken Road, which by now was completely filled with the bodies of nearly 2,600 dead and wounded Confederates. As one Union soldier described it, "In this road there lay so many dead rebels that they formed a line which one might have walked upon as far as I could see. They lay there just as they had been killed apparently, amid the blood which was soaking the earth."[14] In return, the Union's achievement cost them three hours of fighting and almost 3,000 soldiers. General Richardson himself was mortally wounded by Confederate artillery.

< 39 >

At this point, despite their overwhelming losses and many tactical mistakes, the Union forces had a major opportunity to end the battle—and possibly the Civil War—with a decisive victory. Union troops had a chance to take advantage of the huge hole they had put in the Confederate line by pushing D.H. Hill from his position in the Sunken Road. McClellan still had the entire Fifth Corps, as well as much of the Sixth Corps and his cavalry, in reserve. He also had the entire Ninth Corps to the south. If McClellan had committed his forces to completely split Jackson from Longstreet, he could have caught Jackson between the new force and what was left of the First and Twelfth Corps in the North Woods, then turned on Longstreet and trapped him between the Second Corps with the rest of the reserves and the Ninth Corps.

Throughout the battle, however, McClellan was sure that Lee had a much larger force than Lee actually had. Because of this, he remained convinced that most of Lee's force had not yet been used.

The bodies of Confederate soldiers fill the Sunken Road.

Thomas J. "Stonewall" Jackson was probably the second-most-respected man in the Confederacy, after Robert E. Lee himself. Jackson was born in Virginia in 1824. Although he had little formal education, Jackson earned an appointment to West Point. Jackson met Lee while they both served in

Thomas J. "Stonewall" Jackson

Mexico. He married Eleanor Junkin in 1853, but she died the next year. In 1857, he married Mary Anna Morrison.

Jackson earned his nickname at the first battle of Bull Run. As the Confederate troops prepared to retreat, one officer stopped his men by saying, "There is Jackson standing like a stone wall! Rally behind the Virginians!"[15] The Confederates reversed their flight and won the battle. In 1862, he became the hero of northern Virginia and the terror of the Union as he swept through the Shenandoah Valley, where Jackson's 17,000 men were able to defeat 60,000 Union soldiers in a series of forced marches and pitched battles. After capturing Harpers Ferry, Jackson fought at Antietam, Fredericksburg, and Chancellorsville. At Chancellorsville, he was fatally shot in error by his own men as he returned to the Confederate lines at night. Jackson died May 10, 1863.

Therefore, McClellan reasoned, it would be dangerous for him to commit all his reserves to the battle. After capturing the Bloody Lane, McClellan let the fighting in the center and north of the battlefield slow down.

< 41 >

Afternoon Phase

To the south, Burnside was in command of the Ninth Corps. (He was supposed to be in command of the First Corps as well, but it was stationed at the opposite end of the battlefield from the Ninth Corps, and Burnside chose to stay with the Ninth.) Its position was on the extreme left flank of the Union line, and Burnside's duty was to cross Antietam Creek, hit the right side of the Confederate line, and take the town of Sharpsburg.

The area assigned to Burnside's corps was some of the most unfriendly terrain the Union soldiers could imagine. The Rohrbach Bridge (today called Burnside's Bridge) was a stone span 125 feet long and 12 feet wide. A steep hill on the west side of the bridge offered Confederate soldiers a perfect view down onto the bridge, and there was little cover for the Union soldiers as they approached it. Antietam Creek was four to five feet deep in this spot, which was too deep for men to cross while under heavy fire.

Burnside, who was commanding the Ninth Corps with General Jacob Cox, sent one division under General Isaac Rodman downstream to cross the creek and attack the Confederates from their rear. Unfortunately, the crossing selected by Rodman's scouts was not usable—the banks were too steep. Rodman sent his soldiers out to find another crossing. They chose a place two miles from Rohrbach Bridge. Rodman's division would be able to cross there, but it would take much longer than Burnside had anticipated.

When McClellan's orders reached Burnside at 10:00 A.M., he sent the Eleventh Connecticut to attempt a crossing. Using the path along the creek, the regiment was subjected to heavy fire, and they were forced to pull back. One third of their men had been shot.

The Confederates on the other side of the Antietam totaled no more than 520 men, from three Georgia regiments and one company from South Carolina. They were led by General Robert Toombs, and

< 42 >

spread out behind good cover above the bridge. Even though the Union Ninth Corps was made up of 12,500 men, the landscape and narrowness of the bridge gave a clear advantage to the Confederates. The Union officers could only send a limited number of men across at a time, and the Confederates could easily pick them off for as long as their ammunition held out.

Burnside again attempted to cross the bridge by using the path. This attack was led by the Second Maryland. In the space of a few minutes, the regiment suffered 44 percent casualties before abandoning their attempt. To the north, the battle at the Bloody Lane was raging, and General McClellan sent repeated messages to the Ninth Corps to hurry their attack.

Finally, Burnside turned to two regiments of veterans. At 12:30 P.M., the Fifty-First New York and the Fifty-First Pennsylvania, commanded by General Edward Ferrero, were told to storm down the hillside with their combined 670 men and take the bridge. The troops at first were no more successful than the others had been. They were hit by a wave of bullets that halted their charge.

Rather than pulling back, however, the two regiments spread out along the bank of the creek and returned fire. By now the Confederates were starting to run low on ammunition, and under the hail of bullets they were receiving, many started to pull out. Finally, the two Union regiments were able to reach the bridge and race across. Most of the Confederates escaped in time, and those who did not were either killed or captured. It was now 1:00 P.M., and although Burnside had taken his bridge, it was three hours after McClellan had asked him to do so.

Once across the bridge, Burnside had orders to press his attack and relieve pressure in the northern conflicts. Unfortunately, the Ninth Corps was poorly prepared to continue. They needed new ammunition, and their reserve regiments were almost a mile away.

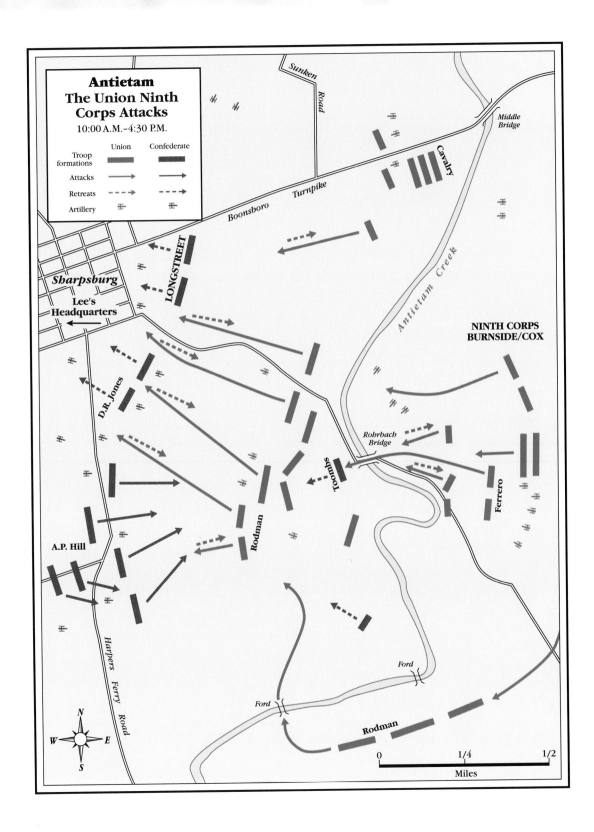

Antietam
The Union Ninth Corps Attacks
10:00 A.M.–4:30 P.M.

Troop formations	Union	Confederate
Attacks		
Retreats		
Artillery		

Sunken Road

Middle Bridge

Cavalry

Boonsboro Turnpike

LONGSTREET

Sharpsburg

Lee's Headquarters

Antietam Creek

NINTH CORPS BURNSIDE/COX

D.R. Jones

Rohrbach Bridge

Toombs

Ferrero

Rodman

A.P. Hill

Harpers Ferry Road

Ford

Ford

Rodman

N
W E
S

0   1/4   1/2

Miles

After suffering many casualties, Union soldiers finally cross the Rohrbach Bridge.

At about 3:00 P.M., the Ninth Corps finally moved to attack the Confederates again. There were 8,500 soldiers in the Union ranks, to oppose the 2,800 Confederate soldiers available to General David Jones. In addition, Burnside had another entire division in reserve, while Jones had no additional infantry left to call on. McClellan himself still had close to 10,000 men who had seen little or no action in the battle. These men were stationed in positions to protect the Union headquarters and supply trains—McClellan still expected Lee to launch some massive counterattack at the Union center.

The Ninth Corps marched forward. Their plan was to take Sharpsburg and cut off Lee's escape to the Potomac. The march proceeded well. Even though the fighting was fierce in many areas, and there were many casualties on both sides, the Union's numbers were enough to push the Confederates back.

A Virginia soldier was one of those forced back under fire: "Oh, how I ran! I was afraid of being stuck in the back, and I frequently turned around in running, so as to avoid if possible so disgraceful a wound."[16] Union soldiers made it all the way to the town of Sharpsburg, and Lee, watching the battle, saw little hope for success. The Confederate wounded were already being moved by ambulances toward the Potomac in expectation of a full retreat.

< 45 >

Marching to the Rescue

Suddenly, as Lee watched, a new cloud of dust arose from the horizon to the south. His concern turned to confidence as he realized that this was not another Union division—it was A.P. Hill's division, marching to the rescue. Hill had been left in charge of the Union surrender at Harpers Ferry. Covering the 17 miles from Harpers Ferry to Sharpsburg in only seven hours, he was able to arrive just in time to turn the tide of the conflict.

One of the first Union leaders to see the danger coming from Hill's division was Rodman, who was killed trying to warn his regiments. As Hill's division attacked the unprotected flank of the Ninth Corps, the Yankee soldiers were slowly pushed back. Suddenly, instead of being on the verge of winning the battle and possibly the war, Burnside's Ninth Corps had to worry about surviving the fight. Pushed almost the entire way back to the bridge, Burnside's corps did eventually hold its ground—but it had lost well over 2,000 men. The Confederates under Jones and Hill had lost about 1,000 soldiers in the fight.

The Cost of the Battle

This finally marked the end of the day's fighting. In terms of land, the Union forces had pushed the Rebel line back one mile on the Confederate left and half a mile on their right. The cost for that very small advance was staggering. The Union lost 12,401 men, who were either killed, wounded, or missing. The Confederacy lost approximately 10,318 men. Both sides lost an astounding number of officers: 20 on the Union side, and 31 on the Confederate. These included 9 Union generals and 9 Confederate generals who were killed or wounded. In all, September 17, 1862, ranks as the bloodiest one-day battle in the history of American warfare.

Born in Liberty, Indiana, in 1824, Burnside was the son of a South Carolina slave owner. He joined the military and graduated from West Point in 1847. In 1852, he married Mary Richmond Bishop.

Ambrose Burnside

At Antietam, Burnside commanded the Ninth Corps. He was blamed for how long it took his soldiers to cross the Rohrbach Bridge. This delay allowed A.P. Hill to arrive in time to save the Confederates from being routed.

Despite what happened at the bridge, Lincoln pressured Burnside to take command of the Army of the Potomac after relieving McClellan from that post. Burnside's command lasted only through his defeat at Fredericksburg. He served as governor and senator of Rhode Island after the war, and died in 1881. Ironically, one of the most lasting contributions Burnside made to history had to do with his odd side whiskers. They were called "sideburns" as a play on his name, and the term is still used today.

Despite their huge losses, the North still had thousands of troops who had not seen any fighting at all and many more who had seen only limited action. The South, meanwhile, had used almost all of its troops in the conflict. Even after all his mistakes and caution, McClellan was obviously in a position to finish the fight the next day, and Lee would be able to do little to stop him.

September 18, 1862, is considered one of the most clearly wasted opportunities to end the Civil War. Union soldiers waited for the

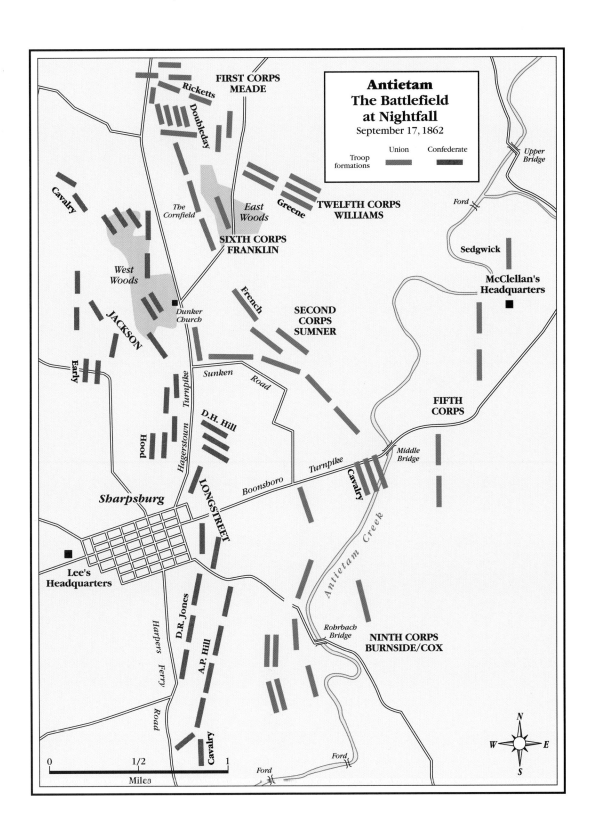

Antietam
The Battlefield
at Nightfall
September 17, 1862

Troop formations — Union — Confederate

FIRST CORPS MEADE

Ricketts

Doubleday

Cavalry

The Cornfield

East Woods

Greene

TWELFTH CORPS WILLIAMS

Upper Bridge

Ford

Sedgwick

McClellan's Headquarters

SIXTH CORPS FRANKLIN

West Woods

JACKSON

Dunker Church

French

SECOND CORPS SUMNER

Early

Sunken Road

FIFTH CORPS

Hood

Hagerstown Turnpike

D.H. Hill

Middle Bridge

Boonsboro Turnpike

Cavalry

Sharpsburg

LONGSTREET

Lee's Headquarters

Antietam Creek

D.R. Jones

Harper's Ferry Road

A.P. Hill

Rohrbach Bridge

NINTH CORPS BURNSIDE/COX

Cavalry

Ford

Ford

0   1/2   1
Miles

N
W   E
S

< 48 >

order to attack, Lee and his men waited for the fight, and President Lincoln and others in Washington, D.C., waited for happy news of the final Union victory. McClellan, however, never gave the order. He was afraid that if his army was defeated, nothing would stand between Lee and the capture of Washington or Baltimore. As night fell, the Army of Northern Virginia withdrew across the Potomac.

The Effects of Antietam

In military terms, the battle of Antietam was considered a draw. Lee's invasion of the North had been halted and turned back, but Lee had also captured Harpers Ferry and left the North with most of his army still intact. Though not a decisive victory for either side, the battle did have a great impact on the remainder of the Civil War.

In Europe, the governments of England and France had considered recognizing the Confederacy as a separate nation and offering assistance. With the failure of Lee's invasion, these governments chose to wait for a more hopeful sign. That sign never came, and the Confederacy never received full recognition from Europe.

In Washington, D.C., President Lincoln was also waiting for a hopeful sign. He had drawn up a statement that he wanted to issue after a clear Union victory. Even though Antietam was not that clear victory, Lincoln decided that pushing Lee back across the Potomac was good enough for his plans. On September 22, President Lincoln issued his preliminary Emancipation Proclamation, declaring freedom for all people living within the areas under rebellion as of January 1, 1863. The proclamation stated that:

All persons held as slaves within any state or designated part of a state the people whereof shall then be in rebellion against the United States shall be then, thenceforth, and forever free; and the executive government of the United States, including the military

Lincoln pays a surprise visit to McClellan (arrow), before relieving him of command.

and naval authority thereof, will recognize and maintain the freedom of such persons.[17]

In effect, President Lincoln had freed slaves who lived in the Confederate states. Lincoln did this for several reasons. By declaring those slaves free, he hoped to weaken the South by possibly inspiring slave rebellions, and forcing the southern armies to worry about protecting their own homes. Lincoln also wanted to regain support of the abolitionists in the North, and remind people that the war was being fought for a strong moral cause, not just territory.

On October 1, 1862, President Lincoln paid a surprise visit to the Antietam battlefield to see General McClellan. The Army of the Potomac had not moved since the battle. McClellan had sent one force to try to cut off Lee's retreat, but they were defeated and returned to Sharpsburg. Lincoln came to Antietam to personally inspect the condition of McClellan's army. Many people in Washington and the North had started to complain about McClellan's failure to move, and Lincoln gave him one last chance to pursue victory. When McClellan still did nothing to follow Lee into Virginia, Lincoln eventually removed him from command. General Ambrose Burnside became the new commander of the Army of the Potomac.

PART THREE

HISTORY REMEMBERED

The Civil War continued for another two and a half years, before General Lee finally surrendered to General Grant at Appomatox Court House in Virginia. Battlefields like Antietam were scattered all over the region from Georgia to Pennsylvania, and west through Tennessee and Kentucky. Places that had been peaceful family farms were forever transformed into graves for the more than 625,000 soldiers who died in the war.

On many battlefields, the winning side was able to remove their dead and send them home for burial, while the side who lost the battle had their soldiers buried where they fell, often in mass graves. Over time, the sites of many of these huge battles and cemeteries were purchased by the U.S. government, and eventually were included in the National Park system. These national parks help to preserve the memories of the fallen soldiers, and of the war that divided them.

Antietam National Battlefield

Today, Antietam National Battlefield is preserved along the same Hagerstown Turnpike (now Route 65) where so many men were killed and wounded on that fateful September day. The park, like all battlefields, is a monument to those soldiers who fought bravely and sacrificed so much. Stories of individual heroism during the Civil War are so plentiful that they could fill their own books. That heroism was shown not only by the soldiers who fought, but by civilians like Clara Barton and all the people of Sharpsburg, Hagerstown, Boonsboro, and other local communities who flocked to help the wounded.

Antietam also stands as a monument to the frustration of those early years of the Civil War. At first, most people thought the war would brief and limited. Battles such as Shiloh made people rethink those assumptions. And although McClellan had several real chances to end the war quickly at Antietam, his failure to do so helped ensure that the Civil War would last several more years.

< 51 >

< 52 >

Antietam is one of the nation's most telling monuments to the terrible cost of war. The nearly 23,000 casualties of America's bloodiest one-day battle are remembered throughout the battlefield itself on plaques and monuments, and in the cemeteries surrounding the area. The dead ranged in age from young teenagers to grandfathers; from drummer boys like 13-year-old Charlie King of Pennsylvania to battle-hardened generals such as Israel Richardson. As Union General Joe Hooker later commented, "it was never my fortune to witness a more bloody, dismal battlefield."[1] Antietam is preserved so that visitors can see the places where so many died: the cornfield, the Bloody Lane, Burnside's Bridge, and others. Photos taken just after the battle show that the landscape was almost the same then as it is today. The National Park system is actively working to replant and restore well-known battle areas such as the West Woods.

Location and Address Antietam National Battlefield, Route 65, one mile north of Sharpsburg, MD. P.O. Box 158, Sharpsburg, MD 21782-0158. Telephone: (301) 432-5124.

Burnside's Bridge, formerly Rohrbach Bridge, still stands at Antietam National Battlefield.

Operating Hours
Daily, 8:30 A.M.–5:00 P.M., Labor Day through Memorial Day, and 8:30 A.M.–6:00 P.M. the rest of the year. The park is open all year except Thanksgiving, December 25, and January 1. September is the busiest month.

Entrance Fees $2 per person; $4 per family. Both are valid for seven days.

Exhibits and Special Events Some 200,000 people come to Antietam National Battlefield every year. Almost the entire area covered by the two armies is preserved as part of the battlefield. It can be viewed

At Antietam National Battlefield, men dressed as the Fourteenth Tennessee wear authentic period costumes.

on foot, by bicycle, or by car. Ranger-guided tours are available. The Visitors' Center at Antietam contains original photos, letters, uniforms, and battlefield relics, such as bullets and cannon shot. There is also a short movie on the battle. Maps, books, and collectors' items can be purchased there. Antietam is also the location of regular Civil War artillery demonstrations and on the first Saturday in December, the annual memorial illumination, when candles are lit across the battlefield in memory of the soldiers who died. Every Fourth of July there is a concert. The 135th anniversary of the battle was marked by a huge reenactment ten miles away from the battlefield itself on September 12–14, 1997.

Thousands of "soldiers" gathered at the Bloody Lane for the 135th anniversary of the battle of Antietam.

Using the Park Antietam National Battlefield is wheelchair accessible in all areas. Restaurants and lodging are available in the towns near Sharpsburg, especially Hagerstown, Maryland, and Shepherdstown, West Virginia. Camping can be arranged for organized groups at the Rohrbach Group Campground. A permit must be obtained at the Visitor Center in order to use the campground. Bicycles and horseback riding are permitted in certain areas.

Harpers Ferry National Historic Park

Harpers Ferry and Antietam offer very different images of the Civil War. Harpers Ferry was attacked because it was an important location for both the Union and the Confederacy. The town represented a stronghold along the border of the two warring sides, and today it is the town itself that is preserved as a National Historic park.

< 55 >

It sits on the West Virginia side of the Potomac River, still surrounded by Loudon Heights, Maryland Heights, and Bolivar Heights, locations which made it possible for Stonewall Jackson to launch his three-part attack from two different states.

Location and Address Harpers Ferry National Historic Park, 20 miles southwest of Frederick, MD, via U.S. 320. P.O. Box 65, Harpers Ferry, WV 25425. Telephone: (304) 535-6223.

Operating Hours Daily, 8:00 A.M.–5:00 P.M. (open until 6:00 P.M. in summer), every day except December 25.

Entrance Fees $5 per vehicle or $3 per person.

Exhibits The town is filled with shops and exhibits, and some of the small shops now serve as museums. One of them describes the lives of freed former slaves in Harpers Ferry, and their status in the United States in the 1860s. There is also an exhibit on some of the weapons manufactured in Harpers Ferry, and a wax museum of famous figures, including John Brown. The engine house where John Brown was captured by Robert E. Lee has been reconstructed.

Union Soldiers on horseback are part of the living history demonstrations at Harpers Ferry.

< 56 >

All around Harpers Ferry are plaques and displays describing John Brown's raid, which helped spark the Civil War, as well as Stonewall Jackson's three-part siege, which was part of Lee's strategy before the battle of Antietam. Hiking trails in the hills surrounding Harpers Ferry trace parts of the attack routes used by Jackson's Confederates. The park offers living history demonstrations and special tours throughout the year.

Related Point of Interest

Manassas National Battlefield Park

The site of two key battles in the Civil War, in 1861 Manassas sent a message to both sides that the war would be longer and more costly than most people assumed. In 1862, it opened the door for Lee's invasion of Maryland and the battle of Antietam.

A statue of Thomas "Stonewall" Jackson, whose determination inspired his men at the first battle of Bull Run, peers out over the battlefield at Manassas.

< 57 >

Location and Address Manassas National Battlefield Park, 26 miles southwest of Washington, D.C., on Route 234 just north of I-66 at exit 47B. 6511 Sudley Road, Manassas, VA 20109. Telephone: (703) 361-1339.

Operating Hours Daily, 8:30 A.M.–5:00 P.M. (open until 6:00 P.M. in summer), every day except December 25.

Entrance Fees $2 per vehicle or $4 per family.

Exhibits The Visitor Center offers exhibits on Civil War uniforms and weapons as well as displays about the two battles fought at Manassas—the first and second battles at Bull Run. There is also an audiovisual battlefield map and a 13-minute slide presentation covering both battles. A walking tour explores the site of the first battle, and an auto tour explores the region where the second battle took place. Ranger-guided tours are also available.

———

Even though the Civil War did not finally end until 31 long months after the battle of Antietam, for many of the men present Antietam remained their clearest memory of the war. In the words of one Pennsylvania captain, "No tongue can tell, no mind conceive, no pen portray the horrible sights I witnessed this morning."[2] The extraordinary violence of the clash, the closeness of the armies, the many heroics of the soldiers, and the decisions and mistakes made by the commanders all combined to represent the best and worst of war at the time. Even the fact that there was no definite winner seems to demonstrate what many found to be true that day and in the months to follow—no one really wins in war. The battlefield at Antietam serves as a constant reminder of that simple and clear fact.

CHRONOLOGY OF THE CIVIL WAR

November 1860	Abraham Lincoln, Republican, elected president of the United States.
December 1860	South Carolina becomes the first southern state to secede from the Union.
February 1861	Six southern states that had seceded form the Confederate States of America.
March 4, 1861	Lincoln sworn in as president.
April 1861	Confederate forces fire on Union Fort Sumter in Charleston, SC and the Civil War begins.
July 1861	Union forces defeated at the battle of Bull Run (First Manassas) in Virginia. First major battle of the war.
February 1862	Forts Henry and Donelson, in Kentucky, captured by Union forces under General Ulysses S. Grant.
April 1862	Battle of Shiloh
August 1862	The second battle at Bull Run (Second Manassas)
September 1862	The siege at Harpers Ferry
	Union forces win control of South Mountain.
	Union soldiers push back Confederate invasion of Maryland at the battle of Antietam (also known as the battle of Sharpsburg).
	Lincoln issues the Emancipation Proclamation, freeing all slaves in Confederate territories.
December 1862	Union suffers massive casualties at the battle of Fredericksburg, in Virginia.
May 1863	Confederates decisively defeat Union forces at the battle of Chancellorsville, Virginia.
July 1863	Grant's army captures Vicksburg, Mississippi.
	Union forces under General George Meade push back the invading Confederate army under

< 59 >

General Robert E. Lee at the battle of Gettysburg, Pennsylvania.

March 1864	General Grant appointed head of all Union forces by President Lincoln.
May-July 1864	Grant's army marches into Virginia and begins a series of bloody battles with Lee's forces across the state from north to south.
August 1864-April 1865	Grant and Lee dig in for a long siege of trench warfare south of Petersburg, Virginia. The siege will last 9 months.
September 1864	General William Tecumseh Sherman captures Atlanta, Georgia. Sherman begins his famous "March to the Sea."
late 1864	Sherman marches through Georgia, burning everything in his path, and reaches Savannah on Christmas Day.
January 1865	Sherman turns north and marches into South Carolina, burning the capital, Columbia, to the ground.
April 1865	Grant breaks through at Petersburg and chases Lee's army into Virginia.
	Richmond, capital of the Confederacy, falls to Union forces. Lincoln enters the Confederate headquarters and sits in Jefferson Davis's chair.
	Lee surrenders to Grant at Appomattox. Lincoln is assassinated a few days later.
May 1865	End of hostilities with the surrender of General E. Kirby Smith of Shreveport, Louisiana
April 1866	President Andrew Johnson declares the Civil War officially over.

FURTHER READING

Bailey, Ronald H. *The Bloodiest Day: The Battle of Antietam.* Alexandria: Time-Life Books, 1984.

Cox, Clinton. *Fiery Vision: The Life and Death of John Brown.* New York: Scholastic, 1997.

Damon, Duane. *When This Cruel War is Over: The Civil War Homefront.* Minneapolis, MN: Lerner, 1995.

Haskins, James. *The Day Fort Sumter was Fired On: A Photo History of the Civil War.* New York: Scholastic, 1995.

Kent, Zachary. *The Battle of Antietam.* Chicago: Children's Press, 1992.

Pflueger, Lynda. *Stonewall Jackson.* Springfield, NJ: Enslow, 1997.

Phillips, Charles. *My Brother's Face: Portraits of the Civil War in Photographs, Diaries, and Letters.* San Francisco: Chronicle, 1993.

Reef, Catherine. *Civil War Soldiers* (African-American Soldiers Series). New York: Twenty-First Century Books, 1993.

Reger, James P. *The Battle of Antietam.* San Diego: Lucent Books, 1996.

Steins, Richard. *Battlefields Across America: Shiloh.* New York: Twenty-First Century Books, 1997.

_____. *The Nation Divides: The Civil War (1820-1880).* New York: Twenty-First Century Books, 1993.

Stiles, T.J., ed. *In Their Own Words: Civil War Commanders.* New York: Berkley Publishing Group, 1995.

Time-Life Books, *Antietam.* Alexandria: Time-Life Books, 1996.

Tracey, Patrick Austin. *Military Leaders of the Civil War.* New York: Facts on File, 1993.

WEB SITES

The World Wide Web is full of information on the Civil War. The American Battlefield Protection Program gives descriptions and summaries of the major conflicts that have taken place on U.S. soil. Their Web address is:

http://www.cr.nps.gov/abpp/abpp.html

For information at that site about the battle of Antietam, the address is:

http://www.cr.nps.gov/abpp/battles/md003.html

Antietam National Battlefield's Web pages are:

http://www.nps.gov/anti/
http://www.nps.gov/ncro/anti/

To locate information about Harpers Ferry, visit:

http://www.nps.gov/hafe/

For information on Manassas, go to:

http://www.nps.gov/mana/

For Union and Confederate Orders of Battle, including casualty numbers, officer listings, and troop deployments, use the following Web pages:

Confederacy: **http://web2.airmail.net/mbusby/sant.htm**
Union: **http://web2.airmail.net/mbusby/nant.htm**

The site called "Antietam—a Photographic Tour" includes photos, maps, descriptions of the battle, and three-dimensional simulations. Its address is:

http://home.ebs.net/~westwood/tour/r_tour.html

The Library of Congress has information on the Civil War at:
http://www.loc.gov

The Library's American history site, called "American Memory," is at:
http://lcweb2.loc.gov/ammem/

SOURCE NOTES

Part One

1. New York *Daily Tribune*, December 3, 1859. Quoted in Thomas A. Bailey and David M. Kennedy, *The American Spirit* (Lexington, MA: D.C. Heath and Company, 1987), p. 409.

2. Don E. Fehrenbacher, ed., *Abraham Lincoln: Speeches and Writings 1859–1865* (New York: Library of America, 1989), p. 256.

Part Two

1. Quoted in Ronald H. Bailey, *The Bloodiest Day: The Battle of Antietam* (Alexandria, VA: Time-Life Books, 1984), p. 15.

2. Ibid., p. 38.

3. Ibid., p. 158.

4. Quoted in Geoffrey C. Ward, *The Civil War: An Illustrated History* (New York: Alfred A. Knopf, Inc., 1990), p. 153.

5. Quoted in Bruce Catton, *The Army of the Potomac: Mr. Lincoln's Army* (New York: Doubleday and Company, 1962), p. 271.

6. Quoted in John Michael Priest, *Antietam: The Soldiers' Battle* (New York: Oxford University Press, 1989), p. 60.

7. Bell Irvin Wiley, *The Life of Billy Yank* (Indianapolis: Bobbs-Merrill, 1952). Quoted in Bailey, *The Bloodiest Day*, p. 429.

8. Quoted in William C. Davis, ed., *The Image of War 1861–1865*, vol. 3, *The Embattled Confederacy* (Garden City, NY: Doubleday and Company, 1982), p. 27.

9. Quoted in Ward, *The Civil War*, p. 158.

10. Quoted in Priest, *Antietam*, p. 85.

11. Quoted in Dr. Jay Luvaas and Col. Harold W. Nelson, eds., *The U.S. Army War College Guide to the Battle of Antietam* (Carlisle, PA: South Mountain Press, Inc., 1987), p. 171.

12. Quoted in Stephen Sears, *The Landscape Turned Red* (Boston: Houghton Mifflin Company, 1983), p. 235.

13. Quoted in William A. Frassanito, *Antietam: The Photographic Legacy of America's Bloodiest Day* (Gettysburg: Thomas Publications, 1978), p. 200.

14. Quoted in Sears, *The Landscape Turned Red*, p. 247.

15. Quoted in Ward, *The Civil War*, p. 67.

16. Ibid., p. 160.

17. Quoted in Henry Steele Commager, ed., *The Heritage of America* (Boston: Little, Brown and Company, 1951), p. 664.

Part Three

1. Quoted in James M. McPherson, ed., *The Atlas of the Civil War*, (New York: MacMillan, Inc., 1994), p. 80.

2. Quoted in Bailey, *The Bloodiest Day*, p. 60.

OTHER SOURCES

Donald, David Herbert. *Lincoln*. New York: Simon & Schuster, 1995.

Dowdy, Clifford, ed. *The Wartime Papers of R.E. Lee*. Boston: Little, Brown and Company, 1961.

McPherson, James M. *Abraham Lincoln and the Second American Revolution*. New York: Oxford University Press, 1991.

Sufakis, Stewart. *Who Was Who in the Civil War*. New York: Facts on File, 1988.

INDEX